FOSSIL FILES

REPTILE
FOSSILS

CHRISTINE HONDERS

PowerKiDS
press.

NEW YORK

Published in 2017 by The Rosen Publishing Group, Inc.
29 East 21st Street, New York, NY 10010

First Edition

Editor: Melissa Raé Shofner
Book Design: Tanya Dellaccio

Photo Credits: Cover De Agostini Picture Library/De Agostini/Getty Images; cover, back cover, p. 1 Victoria Kalinina/Shutterstock.com; p. 5 patarapong saraboon/Shutterstock.com; pp. 6, 17 John Cancalosi/ Getty Images; p. 7 Cameramannz/Shutterstock.com; p. 9 (fossilized algae) Richard Bergman/ Corbis Historical/Getty Images; p. 9 (fly in amber) Wollertz/Shutterstock.com; p. 11 weltreisendertj/ Shutterstock.com; p. 13 sisqopote/Shutterstock.com; p. 15 (*Casineria* fossil) https:// commons.wikimedia.org/wiki/File:Casineria_kiddi.jpg; p. 15 (*Hylonomus* rendering) https:// commons.wikimedia.org/wiki/File:Hylonomus_BW.jpg; p. 19 Alfredo Maiquez/Getty Images; p. 21 Nature/UIG/Getty Images; p. 23 https://commons.wikimedia.org/wiki/File:Museum_of_Natural_ History_Sarcosuchus.jpg; p. 25 (turtle fossil) spatuletail/Shutterstock.com; p. 25 (*Eunotosaurus*) https://commons.wikimedia.org/wiki/File:Eunotosaurus.jpg; p. 27 (*Hadrosaurus* eggs) Jaroslav Moravcik/Shutterstock.com; p. 27 (*Hadrosaurus* skeleton) https:// commons.wikimedia.org/wiki/File:Hadrosaurus_mount.jpg; p. 29 https://commons.wikimedia.org/wiki/ File:Dans_l%27ombre_des_dinosaures_-_Bambiraptor_jeune_-_04.jpg; p. 30 LuFeeTheBear/ Shutterstock.com.

Library of Congress Cataloging-in-Publication Data

Names: Honders, Christine.
Title: Reptile fossils / Christine Honders.
Description: New York : PowerKids Press, [2017] | Series: Fossil files |
  Includes index.
Identifiers: LCCN 2016045963| ISBN 9781499427417 (pbk. book) | ISBN
  9781499429534 (6 pack) | ISBN 9781499428575 (library bound book)
Subjects: LCSH: Reptiles, Fossil–Juvenile literature. | Fossils–Juvenile
  literature.
Classification: LCC QE861.5 .H66 2017 | DDC 567.9–dc23
LC record available at https://lccn.loc.gov/2016045963

Manufactured in the United States of America

CPSIA Compliance Information: Batch Batch #BW17PK: For Further Information contact Rosen Publishing, New York, New York at 1-800-237-9932

CONTENTS

CLUES FROM THE PAST

We know a lot about dinosaurs even though they lived more than 65 million years ago. We know how big they were, what they ate, and even how fast they could run. How do we know so much about them when humans didn't exist when dinosaurs were alive? Much of what we know about prehistoric life is based on what we've learned from fossils.

Fossils contain clues that tell us about the history of life on Earth. They're the **impressions** or preserved remains of **organisms** that lived a long time ago. Fossils have been discovered all over—from the South Pole to the top of the tallest mountain in the world. This book will focus on reptile fossils and what we can learn from them.

Dig It!

The word "fossil" comes from the Latin word *fossilis*, which means "dug up."

Body fossils are the preserved remains of an animal or plant. Footprints and other animal tracks are called trace fossils.

WHAT IS A REPTILE?

The main types of modern reptiles are lizards, snakes, crocodiles, alligators, and turtles. Dinosaurs are examples of ancient reptiles. All reptiles are vertebrates. This means they have a backbone. Reptiles are cold-blooded and can't maintain their own body temperature. They lie in the sun to get warm and then crawl into the shade to cool down. Reptiles are covered with scales and have lungs for breathing. Most reptiles lay eggs.

Scientists believe that the first reptiles existed about 320 million years ago. Their fossils have been found in every part of the world. The reason we know so much about reptiles and how they've changed over time is from studying their fossils.

Tuataras have a third eye on top of their head, but it's covered with scales and it isn't used to see. Scientists think this third eye might help the tuatara know what season or time of day it is.

The Living Fossil

Tuataras are like no other reptiles in the world. They only live in New Zealand, and their closest relatives went **extinct** during the time of the dinosaurs over 60 million years ago. This earned tuataras the nickname "the living fossil." *Tuatara* is a Maori word that means "spiny back." This is fitting because of the spiky scales down the middle of their back. Tuataras are nocturnal, which means they're active at night. They can live for up to 100 years.

HOW FOSSILS ARE FORMED

If an organism becomes buried in sediment soon after its death, it may become a fossil. Sediment is sand, rocks, and other bits of materials that are moved by wind, water, or ice. Over time, more sediment covers the remains and is pressed into solid rock. The organism's soft body parts break down. Water seeps through the rock and minerals in that water slowly replace the bones and other hard parts of an organism that don't rot away. This process takes millions of years.

When the sediment around an organism's remains hardens into rock, it may create a mold. Minerals in the water may fill the mold, creating a cast in the shape of the organism.

This fossilized algae is about 2 billion years old.

Dig It!

Fossils can also be formed in other ways. The remains of small organisms, such as insects, are sometimes found trapped in hardened tree resin called amber. Organisms have also been found frozen in ice. If the ice doesn't melt, organisms may be preserved for thousands of years.

THE STORIES FOSSILS TELL

Fossils tell us about the history of life by showing us how living things have evolved, or changed over time. This history is called the fossil record. In some places, such as the Grand Canyon, you can see the layers of sedimentary rock that formed over millions of years. Each layer represents a different time in history and contains fossils of organisms that lived during that time. By studying each layer, we learn how those organisms evolved.

The fossils of **multicelled** organisms were first found in rock layers from about 550 million years ago. The earliest reptile fossils have been found in rock that is about 320 million to 315 million years old. The younger the rock, the more the fossilized organisms found there look like the plants and animals we see today.

| modern mammals |
| monkeys and apes | **CENOZOIC ERA** |
| early mammals |
| ↑ |
| dinosaurs | **MESOZOIC ERA** |
| ↑ |
| reptiles |
| amphibians |
| jawed fish | **PALEOZOIC ERA** |
| jawless fish |
| invertebrates |

This fossil diagram represents the last 500 million years on Earth. At the very bottom are invertebrates, which are creatures without a backbone. Reptiles first appeared during the late Paleozoic era. The Mesozoic era is known as the "age of the dinosaurs." The Cenozoic era, also called the "age of mammals," is the era we're living in right now.

Grand Canyon

What Else Can We Learn?

We can figure out how old each layer of rock is by knowing what kinds of fossils were found in that layer. The fossil record also tells us how Earth's climate and **environment** have changed over time. If fossils of plants that need warm conditions to live are found in rocks located in the South Pole, that means the South Pole may once have had a very different environment.

THE STUDY OF FOSSILS

Paleontology is the study of plants and animals that lived on Earth long ago. Paleontologists are scientists who learn about the past by studying fossils. They know a lot about geology, which is the study of rocks, and biology, which is the study of life. Paleontologists often use **technology** when they study fossils. For instance, computer models were used to study how the jaws of a *Tyrannosaurus rex* worked and to figure out how hard it could bite. Scientists also used computers when studying the bones of a pterodactyl, an ancient reptile, to learn how it could fly.

Some **engineers** design new tools to make finding fossils easier. They've developed new technology, including a way to create 3-D images from flat fossil imprints.

Young Paleontologists

Kids have made some of the most amazing fossil discoveries. An area full of undiscovered fossils was revealed when two young boys found dinosaur tracks in British Columbia, Canada, in 2001. In 1995, a nine-year-old boy named Michael Arsenault found a fossil on a beach on Prince Edward Island, Canada. The fossil belonged to an ancient reptile that hadn't been discovered before. It's probably 300 million to 250 million years old. In 2015, scientists decided to name the fossil *Erpetonyx arsenaultorum* after its discoverer.

A young girl found the fossil of an ichthyosaur, an ancient marine reptile, in British Columbia, Canada, in 2006. This ichthyosaur fossil is around 180 million years old.

THE OLDEST REPTILE FOSSILS

A creature called *Casineria* may have been the first reptile. Unlike amphibians, it laid its eggs on dry land and may have had scales. Unfortunately, the one *Casineria* fossil that has been found is missing its skull and tail, so scientists aren't sure it's actually a reptile.

The first known reptile is named *Hylonomus lyelli*. The first fossil of this animal was found in petrified wood in Nova Scotia, Canada. *Hylonomus* lived about 315 million years ago and was about 8 inches (20.3 cm) long. It had a lizard-like body and likely ate insects and snails. *Hylonomus* was discovered in 1852 by Sir William Dawson, who named the fossil after a famous geologist, Sir Charles Lyell.

Casineria may have been the first reptile on Earth. Scientists can't know for sure until they find more *Casineria* fossils.

rendering of a *Hylonomus*

Dig It!

In 2007, fossilized reptile footprints were found in a rock layer nearly a half mile (.8 km) below where Dawson discovered his *Hylonomus* fossils. This told scientists that reptiles were older than first thought. Scientists knew the prints were made by reptiles because they had five toes and scales.

MESOSAURUS

The location of the fossils of another ancient reptile, *Mesosaurus*, help explain the idea that the continents were once joined together in one large supercontinent called Pangaea. *Mesosaurus* lived between 299 million and 271 million years ago. It was a crocodile-like reptile about 3.3 feet (1 m) long with a skinny tail and sharp, pointed teeth. It was a freshwater animal that spent most of its time in lakes and ponds.

Mesosaurus fossils have been found only in southern Africa and in eastern South America. Since they were freshwater animals, it would be very unlikely that a *Mesosaurus* swam across the salty ocean from one continent to the other. This supports the idea that Africa and South America were once connected millions of years ago.

The name *Mesosaurus* means "middle reptile." It's an example of a reptile that evolved from land animals but lived most of its life in the water.

THE HISTORY OF LIZARDS

Scientists know that lizards have been around for millions of years, but they haven't always been sure when these creatures evolved. Lizards, snakes, and tuataras are all lepidosaurs and evolved from a common **ancestor**. Until recently, scientists weren't sure when that ancestor first appeared.

In 2013, lepidosaur skull fossils found in Germany helped answer that question. A special dating method was used to figure out how old they were. This method measures the changes in animals' genetic material since the **species** split from their common ancestor. These fossils gave scientists evidence that lepidosaurs were alive 240 million years ago and began to split into different types of modern lizards, snakes, and tuataras around 150 million years ago. The discovery of these fossils was an important

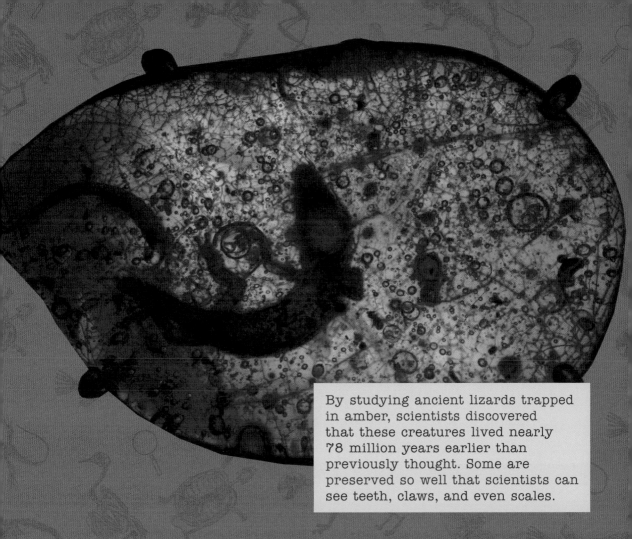

By studying ancient lizards trapped in amber, scientists discovered that these creatures lived nearly 78 million years earlier than previously thought. Some are preserved so well that scientists can see teeth, claws, and even scales.

A Tomb of Amber

In 2016, scientists announced that tiny lizard fossils had been found in Southeast Asia. They weren't like other lizard fossils—they were trapped in amber. Amber is a hardened type of tree resin. The tropical lizards were probably crawling on tree branches when they got stuck in the resin and died. The resin hardened over time, perfectly preserving the unfortunate lizards. The preserved lizards gave scientists more information about these ancient creatures than they'd ever had before.

SNAKES WITH FEET?

The history of snakes is an even bigger puzzle than the history of lizards. The fossil record of snakes is very incomplete because it's hard to find whole fossils of these often small, delicate creatures. So far the oldest snake fossils that have been found are between 167 million and 143 million years old. However, they're just small pieces, so scientists only know that ancient snakes had similar skulls and teeth to modern snakes.

Ancient snake fossils with hind legs were found in rocks that were underwater 100 million years ago. This led scientists to believe that snakes evolved from reptiles that lived in water, such as mosasaurs. Scientists later found a fossil of a land-dwelling snake with hind legs that lived around the same time. It's now believed that snakes evolved from a land-dwelling lizard that hasn't been discovered yet.

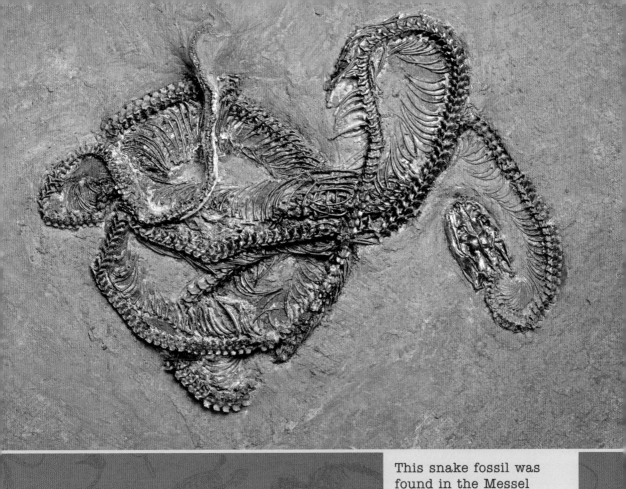

This snake fossil was found in the Messel shale pit in Germany. It's between 56 million and 34 million years old.

Dig It!

The discovery of a 120-million-year-old fossil of a four-legged creature called *Tetrapodophis* has created even more confusion in the snake fossil record. However, some scientists say it's not a snake at all. They claim it's a lizard.

CROCODILIANS

Crocodiles, alligators, and caimans have been around for over 200 million years. They belong to a group called crocodilians. Crocodilians may have changed less than any other reptiles since prehistoric times. However, their fossils still teach us new things.

During a recent dig near the Panama Canal, paleontologists found the skulls of ancient crocodilians. These animals lived 20 million years ago when North America and South America were separated by a seaway, which is a deep waterway. The narrow strip of land that's now Panama didn't surface until millions of years later. The crocodilian skull fossils belonged to relatives of caimans that lived in both North and South America before this land strip existed. Ancient caiman relatives likely used the seaway to travel between continents. This means they swam in salt water, something modern caimans don't often do.

Machimosaurus rex

In 2014, the fossil of a crocodile called *Machimosaurus rex* was discovered in the Sahara Desert. It was 30 feet (9.1 m) long. This 130-million-year-old fossil was the largest marine crocodile ever found. It also represented a new species of teleosaurids, an extinct group of crocodiles. This fossil's existence proved that teleosaurids didn't go extinct about 150 million years ago as scientists previously thought. *Machimosaurus rex* was so large, it could have preyed upon medium-sized dinosaurs.

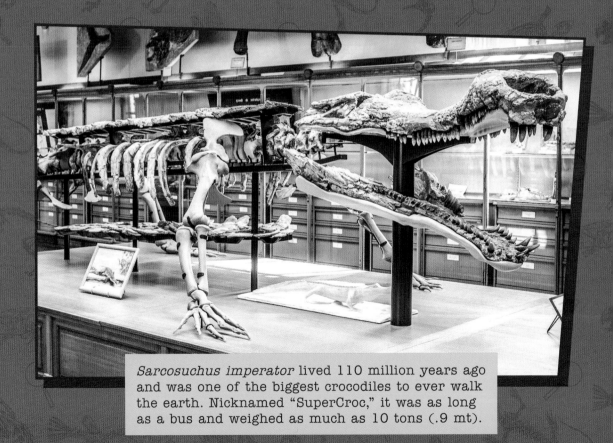

Sarcosuchus imperator lived 110 million years ago and was one of the biggest crocodiles to ever walk the earth. Nicknamed "SuperCroc," it was as long as a bus and weighed as much as 10 tons (.9 mt).

A TURTLE WITHOUT ITS SHELL

One of the most fascinating parts of a turtle is its shell. A turtle shell is made of many fused bones, including ribs and **vertebrae**. Turtles are unlike any other animal in the world because of their shell.

Until recently, the first known turtle fossil with a fully formed shell was 215 million years old. In 2008, fossils of a turtle relative were found in China. It was around 5 million years older than the other fossil. It had a belly shell like a turtle but only a partly formed back shell. In 2013, scientists announced the discovery of *Eunotosaurus*, an older reptile fossil that had similar ribs to modern turtles but no shell. These fossils give scientists new information about the evolution of turtle shells.

In most animals, ribs help with the process of breathing. Turtles' ribs are on the outside of their bodies, so they've evolved to breathe differently. Fossils are helping scientists learn about how the **respiratory systems** of turtles evolved with their shells.

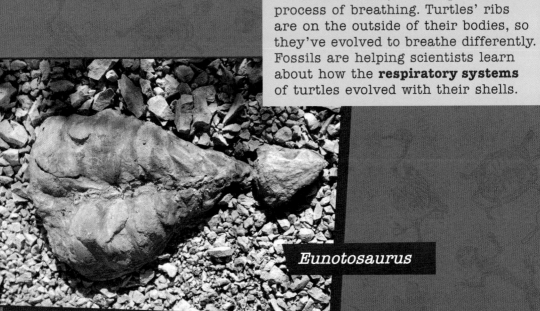

Eunotosaurus

DINOSAUR FOSSILS

Dinosaurs are probably the most fascinating reptiles of all because no one has ever actually seen one. Everything we know about dinosaurs we've learned from fossils.

People found one of the first known dinosaur fossils in 1676. A man who studied it thought it was a bone from a giant human. It was given the name *Megalosaurus* in 1824 by William Buckland, a fossil hunter. *Megalosaurus* lived around 120 million years ago. It weighed about 2,000 pounds (907.2 kg) and likely dined on large animals. In 1842, English scientist Richard Owen examined the *Megalosaurus* fossils and the fossils of two other large creatures known as *Iguanodon* and *Hylaeosaurus*. He realized they all had similarities but were different from any other species. He named this group of animals "Dinosauria," which is

Hadrosaurus eggs

The bones of the *Hadrosaurus* were used by sculptor Benjamin Waterhouse Hawkins to make the first-ever mounted dinosaur skeleton, which was first displayed in 1868.

Dig It!

The first nearly complete skeleton of a dinosaur, later named *Hadrosaurus*, was found in 1858 in New Jersey. This discovery was the first proof that some dinosaurs walked on two legs.

Dinosaur fossils have been found all over the world. They're often divided into two groups: Ornithischia (bird-hipped) and Saurischia (lizard-hipped). Some dinosaurs were covered in a type of body armor, while others had feathers. In fact, their modern-day relatives are birds. Over 1,000 species of dinosaurs have been found and more are discovered all the time.

Scientists can tell from looking at a dinosaur's footprint fossils how many feet it had and how fast it could run. People found some of the largest fossilized dinosaur eggs in China in the 1990s. These eggs measured 24 inches (61 cm) long and 8 inches (20.3 cm) wide.

Scientists also study fossils found inside dinosaurs. Rocks called gastroliths have been found in dinosaurs' stomachs. It's believed they were swallowed to help with **digestion**.

Where Did the Dinosaurs Go?

About 65 million years ago, dinosaurs suddenly disappeared. Scientists aren't sure what happened, but there are many ideas. The supercontinent Pangaea started breaking apart about 200 million years ago. This would have greatly changed the dinosaurs' environment, and they might not have been able to adapt. A giant asteroid hit Earth 65.5 million years ago with the strength of 180 trillion tons (163.3 trillion mt) of explosives. The results of that event may have killed most of the creatures living on Earth.

New fossils can be discovered by anyone. A 14-year-old boy discovered the fossils of this dinosaur, *Bambiraptor*, on his family's farm in Montana. It turned out to be a species no one had ever seen before.

STUDYING FOSSILS

Every new fossil we find tells us a little bit more about the past. By studying fossils, we learn more about what the world was like many years ago and how living things evolved. Fossils also help us work toward a better future by helping us understand how climate has changed and how our behaviors affect our environment.

If you think you might want to be a paleontologist one day, you should study sciences such as biology and geology. You'll learn all about evolution, rock layers, and other important topics that paleontologists need to know. You may also want to volunteer at a science or natural history museum. Always keep an eye out for fossils in rocks. You might discover a new prehistoric species.

GLOSSARY

ancestor: One of the organisms from which another organism is descended.

digestion: The process of breaking down food inside the body so that the body can use it.

engineer: Someone who uses math and science to do useful things, such as building machines.

environment: The conditions that surround a living thing and affect the way it lives.

extinct: No longer existing.

impression: A mark left as a result of applying pressure to something.

multicelled: Made up of many cells.

organism: An individual living thing.

respiratory system: The parts of the body that help in breathing.

species: A group of plants or animals that are all the same kind.

technology: A method that uses science to solve problems and the tools used to solve those problems.

vertebra: One of the bones that make up the backbone. The plural

INDEX

WEBSITES

Due to the changing nature of Internet links, PowerKids
Press has developed an online list of websites related to the
subject of this book. This site is updated regularly. Please use this
link to access the list: www.powerkidslinks.com/ff/rept